IMAGES
of America

AROUND
WARRENSBURG

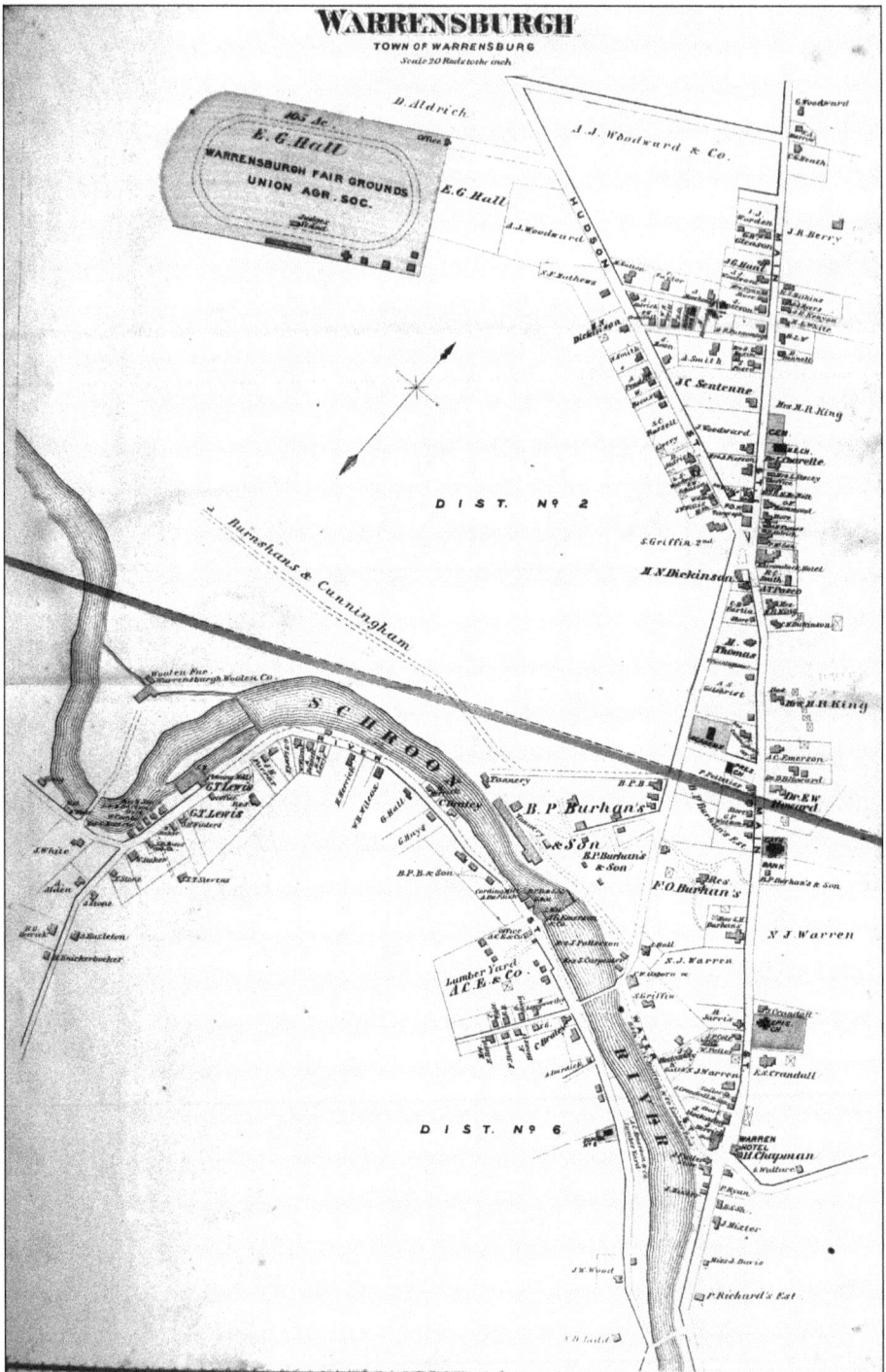

This map of the village of Warrensburgh was taken from Beers Atlas of 1876. (Author's collection.)

On the cover: This 1914 photograph shows three vehicles parked in front of the Grand Army House: a Stanley Steamer, an automobile, and a horse and carriage. (Author's collection.)

IMAGES
of America

AROUND
WARRENSBURG

John T. Hastings in cooperation with
the Warrensburgh Historical Society

ARCADIA
PUBLISHING

Published by Arcadia Publishing
Charleston SC, Chicago IL, Portsmouth NH, San Francisco CA

Library of Congress Control Number: 2009930552

For all general information contact Arcadia Publishing at:
Telephone 843-853-2070
Fax 843-853-0044
E-mail sales@arcadiapublishing.com
For customer service and orders:
Toll-Free 1-888-313-2665

Visit us on the Internet at www.arcadiapublishing.com

This book is dedicated to the many volunteers in the Warrensburgh Historical Society who undertake the many varied activities necessary to promote the history of the community and who have contributed countless hours toward the reopening of the Museum of Local History.

CONTENTS

ACKNOWLEDGMENTS

Like any book of this detail, the final result is a compilation of information and photographs from a wide range of individuals and reference sources. To this end, I would like to thank the following people and organizations.

First of all I would like to thank Sarah Farrar, who provided hard-to-find photographs that came from her grandfather's (Stewart Farrar) collection, as well as the collection at Richards Library. Also her thorough and historical comments from proofreading helped round out many of the descriptions.

Donna Lagoy, Town of Chester historian, provided numerous photographs of locations in and around the village of Chestertown, as well as information on many resorts and businesses that are now a part of history. Her research helped uncover a number of unidentified locations that proved quite helpful to the author.

Also, special thanks to the Warrensburgh Museum of Local History in Warrensburg and the Warrensburgh Historical Society for providing many scarce and hard-to-find images of people and places around Warrensburg.

Thanks to Tom Lynch at the Warren County archives and records who provided early images from the Warren County Highway Department, as well sharing part of his immense knowledge of the county.

Sandi Parisi, Warrensburg town historian, was always there with help and a smile, on any information I was trying to locate.

Other individuals, such as Mark Walp and Lenore Smith, openly provided some unique and interesting images.

Finally, thanks to my brother Roscoe for photographing some of the larger and more difficult images, and Ray Supply in Queensburg for technical photographic assistance.

Also please note that much information was gleaned from the pages of the *Warrensburgh Historical Society Quarterly* (1996–2009) and *A Summer Paradise* published by the Delaware and Hudson Railroad (1896–1942).

Photographs are courtesy of the Warrensburgh Museum of Local History (WMLH), Richards Library (RL), Town of Chester historian's office (TCHO), and Warren County archives (WCA). Unless otherwise noted, all others are from the author's collection.

INTRODUCTION

In 2013, Warrensburg will celebrate its bicentennial. Some 200 years have transformed the village and surrounding area from its original settlement to an industrial community and finally into an area heavily dependent on the tourist trade.

Shortly after the American Revolution, around 1787, William Bond moved to what is now Warrensburg. He settled on lot No. 1 of Hyde Township, and the nearby pond was named in his honor. Later this pond would be renamed Echo Lake. Shortly thereafter, numerous other settlers moved to the area, including Joseph Hutchenson, Josiah Woodward, Stephen Griffing, Joseph Hatch, Richard Thurman, Aaron Varnum, and Dr. McClaren. In 1794, Jonathon Vowers would build the first sawmill on the Schroon River. Nineteen years later, the Fox brothers would be the first to float logs down the Schroon River to the mills in Warrensburg and Glens Falls. Other small-scale industries, such as a gristmill and tannery, would soon be established. It was on February 12, 1813, that the town was established. Unfortunately, Bond, who was living in Chestertown, would pass away early the same year and not see the formation of the town.

Located near the junction of the Schroon and Hudson Rivers, these waters provided Warrensburg with the necessary power and transportation needs to move the goods and materials of a growing community. Further transportation development in the area such as the Feeder Canal in Glens Falls in 1832 and the Plank Road from Glens Falls to Chestertown (1848–1850) would provide additional means of moving products to the Glens Falls and lower Hudson areas. The period after the Civil War would see the greatest development of Warrensburg industries, as the Burhans tannery, Emerson sawmill and sash and blind mill, Foster peg factory, the shirt factory, and the woolen mill and pants factory were all either established or greatly enlarged during this time. The rivers provided the power, and the forest provided the raw materials. With the improved transportation network, the resulting products could be shipped worldwide.

As the 20th century dawned, many of these factories and mills would be gone. Only the Emerson sawmill, shirt factory, and woolen mill would remain. With the advent of the automobile, people were able to move around and vacation like they had never done before. Previously it would take a day or more to travel by train from New York City to the Adirondacks, where they would vacation in one spot for weeks or the entire summer. By the early 1900s, people could drive north on Route 9 and be at their favorite spot in a matter of hours and then move on to different locations over the period of their vacation. The Adirondacks were no longer open to just the rich.

With people anxious to vacation in the clean, unspoiled environment of the Adirondacks, the tourist industry had begun. Early brochures note the clean springwater, pure air, and fresh vegetables to be had at their establishment. Later, in the 1930s and early 1940s, dude ranches became the rage. Many ranch and resorts opened in Warrensburg, Stony Creek, Luzerne, and Thurman. Such marked the transformation of Warrensburg and many other Adirondack towns from industrial-based communities to villages relying on the resort and tourist trades. Hotels, motels, and boardinghouses started to grow in numbers. Dude ranches, amusement parks, golf courses, and other recreational facilities were soon developed. After the end of World War II, the transformation was nearly complete; the Adirondacks had become one of the major tourist destinations for people living on the East Coast, and Warrensburg became known as the "Queen Village of the Adirondacks." (Note: In some cases the author will be using the older spelling of Warrensburg when referring to a specific name. The current spelling often does not include the *h* at the end, as a result of a post office decision in the 1890s.)

The town of Chester is located just north of Warrensburg between the Hudson and Schroon Rivers. It was set off from the town of Thurman on March 25, 1799, and was part of Washington County until Warren County was established in 1813. The main settlement was first known as Wabir and later as Chester Four Corners until the post office was established around 1808. At this point it became known as Chestertown.

Three lakes are located within or adjacent to the town, Loon, Friends, and Schroon. These, along with the Hudson and Schroon Rivers, provided an abundant water resource for early transportation of agricultural and forest products.

Many of the first settlers were given grants of land for their service in the Revolutionary War. These included Seba Higley, Martin Vosburgh, Peleg Tripp, and the Van Benthuysens. Other early settlers left their names as landmarks in various areas of the town: Landon Hill, Starbuck Hill, Darrowsville, and Tripp Lake.

Rev. Jehiel Fox organized the first Baptist church in the town around 1796. Later his two sons Norman and Alanson became noted for instituting the first use of rivers (Schroon) to transport logs to the mills in Warrensburg and Glens Falls in 1813. Logs for this first river drive came from the Brant Lake Tract.

Transportation and access improved with the construction of the Warrensburgh and Chester Plank Road in 1850 and the completion of the suspension bridge across the Hudson River at Riverside in 1874. These allowed better movement of agricultural and forest products to the mills and population centers to the south, as well as movement of "sports" and tourists to the north.

From 1850 to 1885, the prime industries in the town were the C. F. Faxon Tannery and gristmill. Other smaller industries were present, such as a limestone quarry, J. M. Stone stone works, Parker Carding Mill, White and May harness and collar making, Pickens wheelwright, Aranda Barber cooperage, and a small shirt factory operated by Bishop Phelps, who obtained waists from the J. P. Baumann factory in Warrensburg. Phelps also had a sawmill, planning mill, and gristmill, which operated in the late 1870s and early 1880s. By 1900, most of these had closed, however, leaving the way open for the development of tourism.

The water that moved raw materials to the markets now attracted "sports" to the mountains to hunt, fish, and undertake other forms of recreation in a clean, quiet environment not found in the heavily industrialized cities of the East Coast. As with other North Country villages, a new era of tourism and movement of "live hides" had begun.

Such is the purpose of this book, to show how small towns in the Adirondacks have made this transformation. Whether visitors are going skiing, hiking, golfing, hunting, fishing, or attending the World's Largest Garage Sale or Stone Bridge Caves, they continue to discover the hidden gems nestled in the mountains of northern New York . . . Warrensburg and Chestertown.

One

MAIN STREET

Then, as now, Main Street contained most of the retail shops, churches, and major hotels. Much of the street was lined with large elms and maples, as can be seen in this early photograph. Dutch elm disease, salt damage, and widening of Route 9 has eliminated most of these trees over the years.

Entering the village from the south in the early 1900s, one encountered two bridges, located side by side across the Schroon River. One bridge was for the trolley, and the second was the Plank Road Bridge for vehicular traffic. The first trolley entered Warrensburg in January 1902. Coupon booklets could be obtained for $7.50, which included 200 5¢ rides. A round-trip to Glens Falls cost 75¢. (RL.)

The plank road was built between 1849 and 1850. The first section was from Glens Falls to Lake George, with subsequent sections to Lake George and then Warrensburg and finally to Chestertown. The efforts of four of Warrensburg's prominent businessmen, Thomas Gray, Peletiah Richards, Joseph Woodward, and Benjamin Burhans, resulted in the plank road being built.

The Judd Bridge crosses the Schroon River on the southwesterly side of the town. The bridge was named for Samuel Judd, who owned a large tract of farmland on the opposite hillside. The first bridge was built by Timothy Stowe around 1820. In February 1923, as Ben Guiles and Walter Varnum were hauling a load of wood over the bridge, it collapsed. The weight of the horses, men, and wood was too much for the 30-year-old bridge. Walt, along with his grandfather, had the dubious honor of also going through the previous Judd Bridge. Replacement of the bridge occurred the following year with an iron structure. (Above, WCA.)

The Trimble Hotel was located just north of the High Rock and across from the Judd Bridge. Originally it was known as the Riverside Hotel. After Stephen Waters purchased it in 1905, he renamed it the Trimble Hotel. He eventually sold it in 1909. Later it was known as the Bolton Hotel, Kelly's Inn, and when it burned in 1926, as the Ah-kum-on Inn.

Above is a photograph of the interior of the Trimble Hotel. After purchasing the hotel, Stephen Waters built a bowling alley as part of the hotel.

As one entered the village, the High Rock stood on the right side of the road across from the Judd Bridge. This was a glacial erratic left as the last glaciers melted and receded north. The rock was dynamited and removed in 1930 to widen Route 9. About the time of its removal, the Warrensburg High School adopted the name *Hi-Rock* for the title of its school newspaper. (WMLH.)

The Warrensburgh Garage was at one time located just north of the Warren House and then later near the Judd Bridge. In July 1915, the garage kept track of the number of cars that passed by. For an eight-hour period, 584 cars passed the garage, or 73 per hour. (WMLH.)

Later on, the Warrensburgh Garage was located on lower Main Street. From around 1931 until 1946, it was run by James Hastings and Hollis Ovitt. In 1935, it was destroyed by fire but was rebuilt. The photograph shows the interior of the garage with James Hastings on the right and his brother Willis "Buster" Hastings on the left.

The Mixters were one of the earlier families to settle in Warrensburg. John Mixter was a blacksmith and in 1879 became supervisor of the Town of Warrensburg. Records indicate that in 1816 the ground floor of this building was a blacksmith shop, and the second floor was magnificently furnished as a ballroom. From the 1920s on, the building was used as an antique shop.

The Swan House (located in the background of this photograph) is located on the southeast corner of the Horicon Avenue and Route 9 intersection. Patrick Ryan established a shoemaking business at this location after coming here from Ireland in the 1870s. He specialized in children's boots and calked shoes, which were used by the lumbermen during the river drives.

The Grand Army House was purchased in 1887 by Patrick Heffron. Prior to this, it was known as the Fuller Boarding House. Heffron remodeled and enlarged the boardinghouse in 1893, and it was officially named the Grand Army House in honor of Heffron's service in the Union army. In 1929, the hotel was badly gutted by fire. It was near this time that the name was changed to the Warren Inn.

The Warren Inn was located on the site of the original Grand Army House. It was built after the previous hotel was destroyed by fire in 1929. It was also known as Linindolls. The site is currently occupied by George Henry's tavern and is located on the southwest corner of Main Street and River Street.

LININDOLLS HOTEL, WARRENSBURGH, N.Y.

16

The Warren House was near where the current Stewart's Store is located. James Pitt first built and ran a tavern on this site in 1789. James Warren bought the hotel in 1804, and the family ran it until 1866. It was destroyed by fire in 1888, rebuilt in 1892 by Alfred Brown, and then burned again in 1921. This picture was taken in the early 1900s.

The Crandall Block was located on lower Main Street across from the Warren House. The building was constructed in 1896 by Emerson Crandall, who was heavily engaged in the mercantile business. Crandall was a long-term resident of the village and served as justice of the peace, town clerk, and county treasurer and was postmaster from 1894 to 1898. Much of this area burned in a disastrous fire in February 1927.

The top view is looking north from in front of the Warren House. This area was often referred to as the "lower borough" or "downtown." The lower view is a hearse (possibly Woodward Undertakers) in front of the Dickinson and Bertrand's Pharmacy. G. W. Dickinson had started the business in 1877. After the store was destroyed in the 1927 fire, Dickinson retired, and Henry Bertrand established the business in the Music Hall Block.

This picture was taken in front of the International Order of Odd Fellows (IOOF) hall during the Rebekahs' centennial celebration (1934). The hall was built in 1926 and dedicated the following year. Warrensburg Lodge No. 488 was instituted in 1881. In the photograph are, from left to right, Anna Farrar, Lillian Weaver, Rita Culver, Bertha Hill, Clarabelle Wells, Belle Hayes, Myrtle Hull, Abbie Davis (Hastings), Elda Davis (Monroe), Mildred Johnson, Evelyn Brown, Rosale Washburn, and Hazel Noble. (Abbie Hastings.)

The above photograph shows the parade float of the Rebekahs' during the centennial celebration. In back is the IOOF hall, which now houses the Warrensburgh Museum of Local History and the VFW Haskel Brothers Post 482. In the photograph are, from left to right, Laura Barlow, Flossie Hayes, Irene Pratt, Lillian Weaver, and Rita Culver. (Abbie Hastings.)

The 5th United States Infantry marches through Warrensburg in 1906 after returning from training in Camp Gretna, Pennsylvania. They would spend the night at the fairgrounds before continuing their march back to Plattsburgh. The view is looking northward on lower Main Street. The Episcopal church is on the right just out of view.

The Episcopal church was built in 1864 by local builder Albert Alden, descendant of the famous John and Priscilla Alden. Stone for its construction was quarried from Hackensack Mountain. In 1865, the church tower and porch were added, and when the tower was completed, a bell weighting 627 pounds was presented to the parish by Col. B. P. Burhans. The parish house and rectory were built in 1886, and the cloister was added in 1911.

The Elms (later the Pillars) adjoined the Burhans Mansion property. It was formerly the home of Thomas S. Gray, who at the time was a partner with Colonel Burhans in the tannery business. Later it was the home of Clara Richards and Mary (Richards) Kellogg, who donated the land and funds for the construction of Richards Library.

The Burhans Mansion was erected in 1865 by Colonel Burhans for his son Frederick. That summer, activities at the tannery were practically suspended, and most of the 150 employees were engaged in the construction of the mansion. The stone came from Hackensack Mountain, and Albert Alden was the head mason. In 1865, Colonel Burhans resided in the adjoining house and with his son operated the tannery. (WMLH.)

Catholic Church, Warrensburgh, N. Y.

St. Cecelia's Catholic Church was built in 1874 through the efforts of Rev. James A. Kelly, a pioneering clergyman who traveled throughout much of Warren County. The cornerstone was laid on July 23, 1875. The 1,000-pound bell was cast in the famous Meneely Foundry at West Troy.

Albert C. Emerson was eight years old when his father, James, and mother, Polly (Wells), moved from Newbury, New Hampshire, to Warrensburg in 1837. In 1855, he married Abigail Woodward and bought the Samuel Richards home (above). It was near this time that he entered the lumber business, which eventually became A. C. Emerson and Company. He had two sons, James and Louis.

Dr. Daniel Howard had this house built shortly after the Civil War. Dr. Howard graduated from Albany Medical College in 1865 and returned to Warrensburg to become a partner with his father. His father was Dr. Eliakim W. Howard, who moved to Warrensburg in 1837. During the Civil War, Dr. Eliakim Howard was appointed examining surgeon for the pension office and held this position for many years. (RL.)

The Thomas Cunningham law office was built around 1862 by Moses Sutton. It was also used by Arthur Cunningham as a dental office and was removed to the Robert Cunningham property on Library Avenue in 1931. Thomas Cunningham, who moved here in the 1850s, lived in the house in the background. These buildings were located just north of Stewart Farrar Avenue. (RL.)

Baptist Church,
Warrensburgh, N. Y.

The First Baptist Church of
Warrensburg had 43 members in 1809.
Members met at various locations
over the years, until September 1877,
when construction of the church
was completed at a cost of $6,800. In
August 1917, the steeple was struck by
lightning, and then on January 1, 1997,
the church was completely destroyed
by fire.

The New Emerson National Bank
Warrensburg

The Emerson National Bank was founded in 1883 by Albert C. Emerson and known as Emerson
and Company, Bankers. The first bank was located at the corner of Main and Hudson Streets.
Later it moved to the Adirondack Hotel before eventually moving to the building shown above,
after its construction in 1927. In 1936, Albert L. Emerson was elected president and served until
his death in 1963.

The King House, later the Gilchrist Manor, was built by Peletiah Richards in the early 1800s. This house was one of the few examples of Southern Colonial architecture in the North Country. The mansion of a Southern planter caught the eye of Richards, and he sent a local builder to Virginia to measure the house and to create a replica in Warrensburg. Hesden King, Richards's son-in-law, bought the house from him, and in May 1941, it was purchased by Paul Gilchrist from the estate of Frederick King, Richards's grandson. The lower picture shows the King family outside their home. (WMLH.)

The bandstand in Floyd Bennett Memorial Park was used both for concerts and as a focal point in the community. The Warrensburg community band would often play here. The above view was taken shortly after the bandstand was completed. In the background of the view below can be seen the Colonial Arms and Hackensack Mountain.

Floyd Bennett r...
Warrensburg, N.Y.

In 1929, American Legion Post 446 erected a flagpole with a bronze tablet on the base at the north end of the park in memory of Floyd Bennett. It was at this time that it became known as Floyd Bennett Memorial Park. Bennett was the navigator for Adm. Richard E. Byrd when he flew over the North Pole. He died in 1928. The photograph above shows Bennett's mother raising the flag at the dedication ceremony and his wife, Caroline, giving the memorial address in the photograph below.

rs. Caroline L. Be...ett ...ivering Memorial address
Floyd Bennett ...die... ...n Warrensburg, N.Y.

The Adirondack Hotel was originally built around 1825. The photograph above shows the hotel in the 1880s after several additions. Two fires, 1889 and 1895, destroyed this and a subsequent building. It was rebuilt again in the late 1890s and called the New Adirondack Hotel (photograph below). Owners over the years have been Edmund Richards (brother to Peletiah), Alton Nelson, Joseph Woodward, John McClaren, Bradford Tubbs, Stephen Griffing, Lewis Persons, Royal Smith, and the Hammonds.

Colonial Arms Wa

In 1939, the Adirondack Hotel was purchased by Albert L. Emerson and renamed the Colonial Arms. It was at this time that the famed horseshoe bar was created. Later it was owned by Marcus Bruce and Jack Casey. In the 1970s, fires destroyed much of the rear section, including the bowling alleys and swimming pool. In 1994, the property was purchased by a developer, demolished, and replaced with a modern drugstore chain.

Hammonds Crystal Pharmacy stood on Main Street at the north end of the present-day gas station owned by Jack Toney. It was owned by Oscar Hammond and opened in 1862. He and his wife, Holly, lived in the house next door, which is still standing. At one time, Oscar and his son Fred also owned the Adirondack Hotel. Oscar died of Bright's disease in 1897. (WMLH.)

The top floor of the Aldrich-McGann block was known as the Music Hall. The second Music Hall burned in 1895 along with the Adirondack Hotel and Hammond's Pharmacy. It was rebuilt in the late 1890s and succumbed again to fire in December 1950. It was used for plays, dancing, and even basketball. The first floor contained stores and offices and was also the original home of Oscar's Meat Market from 1943 to 1950.

Trilby Cottage was the name given to Hod Hill's and Kid Manzer's barbershop. Hill sold the shop to Manzer around 1901 but returned as a partner in 1903. Louise Tubbs believes it stood in back of the Music Hall. From left to right are Dr. Billie D. Aldrich, Abie Ginsburg, Jim Mulligan, Will Haley, Myron Shaw, Berry Woodward, Seth Reed, Horatio Goodman, unknown, Barney Hammond, Ernest "Kid" Manzer, Ed Beaupre, John L. Tubbs, and Guy St. Marie. (RL.)

The Woodward Block was the name of the large stone building across the street from the bandstand. The building is well over 150 years old and has housed numerous businesses, including a telegraph office, post office, jewelry store, insurance company, and garage. The upper floor, built by Albert Alden, once served as the lodge for the Masons. The first floor was built by Peter Buell. Note the McNutt fountain in the right foreground.

This panoramic view of the Woodard Block, Music Hall, and Adirondack Hotel was taken from the north end of Elm Street, with Hackensack Mountain in the background. Note the early automobile in the lower left corner. This area was often referred to as the "upper borough,"

"uptown," or "Hampshire." The later name came from the Emerson family because it reminded them of their native New Hampshire.

The northern end of the trolley line came to where the Woodward and McGann blocks stood, at which point there was a turnaround. The trolley began operation in 1902 and continued until 1927. The photograph shows the trolley, with a plow attached, clearing the tracks near the Music Hall.

This view is looking north on Main Street after a heavy snowstorm in March 1900. The photograph was taken near Hammond's Crystal Pharmacy and the West Law Office on the east and the J. G. Hunt's on the west. In the photograph are Thomas McGann, Ben Hammond (proprietor), Fred Hammond, and Harry Clark (druggist). (WMLH.)

34

A crew from the Warren County Highway Department is shown removing snow on Main Street in the 1920s. The lack of a cab on the truck had to make for cold work. The Music Hall and Hammond's Crystal Pharmacy are on the right. (WCA.)

A view looking north on Main Street includes Hammond's Crystal Pharmacy on the right and to the left of the parked car, the J. G. Hunt's hardware store, which is now Marco Polo's Pizza. The Woodward Block is at the very left edge of the photograph. A sign in the background advertises gas at 20¢ a gallon.

The home of Thomas McGann is located on Main Street just north of the Woodward Block. McGann served as a hotel clerk at the Rising House in Chestertown, and in 1898, he went into the dry goods business with his brother Henry. Eventually he became part owner in the Aldrich-Thomson Block. He served as town clerk for two terms and collector for one. Later this would become the law office of John S. Hall.

This was the home of Helen Somerville and is the second house north of Jacob's and Toney's. In 1920, Somerville traded the Dickinson home (see page 38) to her aunt for this house. Helen's mother, Grace, was the daughter of Myron Dickinson. Grace was married to James M. Somerville, who was publisher of the *Warrensburgh News* (1890–1917) and superintendent at the Empire Shirt Company.

The John G. Hunt house was built before 1876 and enlarged in 1888. Hunt came to Warrensburg in 1871 and operated a wholesale and retail hardware store. Hunt had a fondness for fine horses and raised several Morgan steeds on a farm on the Schroon River Road.

The Methodists were the first to form a church organization in Warrensburg (1796). A portion of the structure at 166 Main Street is the original Methodist church building, which was moved there from its original site. A second structure was built in 1840 and then moved to King Street so that the current church could be built in 1904. The parsonage is the building to the left of the church.

In 1857, Myron Dickinson built a sawmill in Warrensburg and then moved to the village. It was near this time that the above house was built. During the Civil War he served as captain in the 118th New York Volunteers. After the war he opened a mercantile store, from which he retired in 1871 and started a book/stationery business. His granddaughter Helen Somerville is standing on the lawn, with Dickinson seated on the porch. (WMLH.)

Rice's Guest House was originally built in the 1890s by Lewis Thomson. It was passed on to his only heir, Pearl Rice, who, with her husband, owned the Brown Swan Club in Schroon Lake. The name came into being during the 1930s. Later it was run as the Bent Finial Manor, and currently it is operating as the Cornerstone Victorian.

Bonnie Brae Villa was built in 1865 by Capt. John Russell after he returned from the Civil War, with his southern bride, Mary Denison. He died in 1909. The house was purchased by Kate Parker in 1920 and operated as a summer boardinghouse. Later Hilda and Willie Muller renamed it the Chalet Swiss, an upscale restaurant and guesthouse that they operated until they retired. The house burned March 13, 1980, in a spectacular fire.

Len's Cabins was owned by Len Harrington and was in operation in the 1930s and into the 1950s. Besides cabins, there were also camping sites. Notice the enclosed and shaded viewing areas built into the stone wall along the road and the donkey in the right center of the lower photograph. It was located at the north end of Main Street. Len's wife was Myrtle, and they lived on Herrick Avenue. Len also ran a trucking service during the 1920s and 1930s.

Two

RIVER STREET

Norman and Alanson Fox were the first to undertake the river driving of logs on the Schroon River in 1813. White pine logs harvested on the Brant Lake Tract were floated down the Schroon and Hudson Rivers to the mills in Warrensburg and Glens Falls. Other loggers followed suit, and for the next 140 years, rivers became the primary means to move softwood logs to the mills farther south.

Most industry and mills were located along the Schroon River, as this provided a source of transportation and waterpower. River Street parallels the river on the south side. This view shows the Emerson lumberyards with the shirt factory in the background. The train, in the foreground, came to the village in 1906. (RL.)

The Riverview House or Lodge was located on the south side of the Schroon River just below the Osborne Bridge. Frank Cunningham was the proprietor from 1909 to 1923. In 1924, Harold Turpin took over and ran it as the Riverside Lodge until around 1930 when E. J. Waters became owner and ran it as the Riverview Lodge.

The Osborne Bridge is the third bridge to cross the Schroon River as one approaches the village from the south. In 1882, this bridge was impassable, and people going to or coming from Lewisville had to "walk the plank" to get to the east side of the river. The iron bridge was built in 1887, and the current bridge was built in 1933. This view is looking westerly over the bridge, with the Woodward home in the right center of the photograph. (WCA.)

The David Woodward home was located on River Street near the Osborne Bridge. David's father was John Woodward, grandson of one of the early settlers of Warrensburg. David served in the 118th New York Volunteers during the Civil War. Later he became a member of the firm of A. C. Emerson and Company and also served on the board of education for the Union Free School from 1888 to 1892. (WMLH.)

The Emerson Sawmill was built by Dudley Farlin (1818), who later (1834) sold it to Nelson Warren. After undergoing various ownership changes, in 1872 it became A. C. Emerson and Company. In 1927, it was bought by D. E. Pasco and Sons. It was a gang mill, containing over 70 saws and 4 gates, requiring 3 wheels for power. The early mill had an annual capacity of nearly three million board feet of lumber. (Stewart Farrar collection.)

Looking northwesterly from the Osborne Bridge is the Emerson Sawmill on the left and the smaller Smith Sawmill on the right. The shirt factory appears in the far left. Just beyond the Smith Mill was the first electric light station, which was constructed in 1894 by John G. Smith. At the time, it was one of the most thoroughly equipped light plants in New York State. In 1915, he sold the business to M. L. Runner.

The Empire Shirt Factory was established and built in the fall of 1879 by Louis Weinman and Louis Emerson. By 1882, James Emerson became the sole owner. In 1891, it was taken over by J. P. Bauman and Son, and the production of ladies shirtwaists was initiated. By 1896, production was noted at 500 dozen waists and 200 dozen night robes daily. Over 800 people were employed. The shirt factory was in production until around 1960. (Above, WMLH.)

The first sole leather tannery in Warren County was the Warren Tannery in Warrensburg. It was built in 1831 by H. S. Osborn and Company. The original owners did not succeed, and the tannery was taken over by H. J. Quakenbush in 1834. It went through various joint ownerships, including Quakenbush and (Thomas) Gray, Burhans and Gray, and Burhans, Gray,

and Company, over the next 25 years. In 1860, Col. B. P. Burhans bought out Gray, whereby the company changed to B. P. Burhans and Sons. Although Colonel Burhans died in July 1875, his heirs continued to run the tannery for 10 years, until it closed in 1885. The tannery had a capacity of about 3,500 hides per year. (Stewart Farrar collection.)

Originally the D. E. Pasco Hardware store, grain storehouse, and gristmill were owned by B. P. Burhans and Sons. Thomas Smith of Horicon was the manager (1882) and later (1886) owner of the gristmill. It was turned over to his son Frank Smith, who then sold it to Delbert E. Pasco around 1927. Delbert died in 1948, and his son Walter took over. Walter's son Delbert H. Pasco and nephew Robert Pasco would eventually become owners. (WMLH.)

Herrick's Variety Store was established in 1893 by James Herrick. Initially it was a carriage shop, but when a fire destroyed the shop in 1912, the remainder of the building was left as a general store, which continued operation until around 2000.

The section along lower River Street, from the Osborne Bridge to where the sidewalk ends, was known as Lewisville. Around 1900, the area experienced a housing boom along the south side of the river and was often referred to as the "Klondike." Fred Cunningham was the seller of many of these lots. This view is looking west toward the Three Sisters Mountains.

The current Woolen Mill Bridge was constructed around 1898, although the original bridge existed prior to 1876, when the woolen mill was first constructed. It is a one-lane bridge that spans the Schroon River and connects Milton Avenue to River Street. The photograph was taken around 1911. This bridge is currently being considered for replacement. (WCA.)

The Warrensburgh Woolen Mill and Pants Factory was built by R. G. Herrick in 1873 at a cost of $3,650. Around 1894, production was doubled with the building of an addition and the adjacent dam. In 1885, James Emerson and T. J. Eldridge became the owners. Production gradually increased from 60 to 250 pairs of pants per day. All operations were suspended in 1939. These woolen blankets and pants were known throughout the Northeast for their quality and durability. (Below, RL.)

The Wayside Hotel was originally opened in 1889 and was owned and operated by Martin Griffin. It has gone through various ownerships over the years, including Halsey Truesdale, Herbert Wood, and George Glassbrook. It is located just west of the Woolen Mill Bridge on the south side of the Schroon River. The building is still present and owned by Charles Bedarian.

The Foster shoe peg factory was built in 1882 by Wyman Flint and later owned by J. R. Foster. Blue Star shoe pegs were manufactured from white birch, and up to 20 barrels were made daily. Many were shipped to Germany for its army. The factory closed in 1893, and the building burned in 1898. Contributing to its demise was the loss of 123 barrels of shoe pegs in 1892 when the steamship *Eider* ran aground. (RL.)

The sash and blind factory was built downstream from the shoe peg factory by John Brill. Later it was owned by G. T. Lewis, who sold the property to Stephen and Walter Pasco (1873) with the company name of S. Pasco and Brother. They ran the business until 1896, when it was sold to Delbert Pasco and George Davison. The mill burned in 1899, was rebuilt, and then was destroyed again in 1907. (WMLH.)

In 1871, Thomas Durant constructed the first railroad north along the Hudson River to North Creek. However, it was not until 1905 that a spur line was built into Warrensburg by the contractors Charles Hart and John Cameron, who were from New Jersey. A train passes through the Lewisville area of Warrensburg in midwinter with Hackensack Mountain in the background. This section was abandoned by the Delaware and Hudson Railroad in 1980. (WMLH.)

52

The Schroon River Pulp and Paper Company was incorporated in 1892. Up to 10,000 market logs (approximately two million board feet) of spruce and aspen were utilized to produce a high-quality ground wood pulp each year. The dam was 175 feet wide and had a drop of 24 feet, which could produce waterpower of up to 2,000 horsepower. The mill was closed, and the dam went out in 1976. (WMLH.)

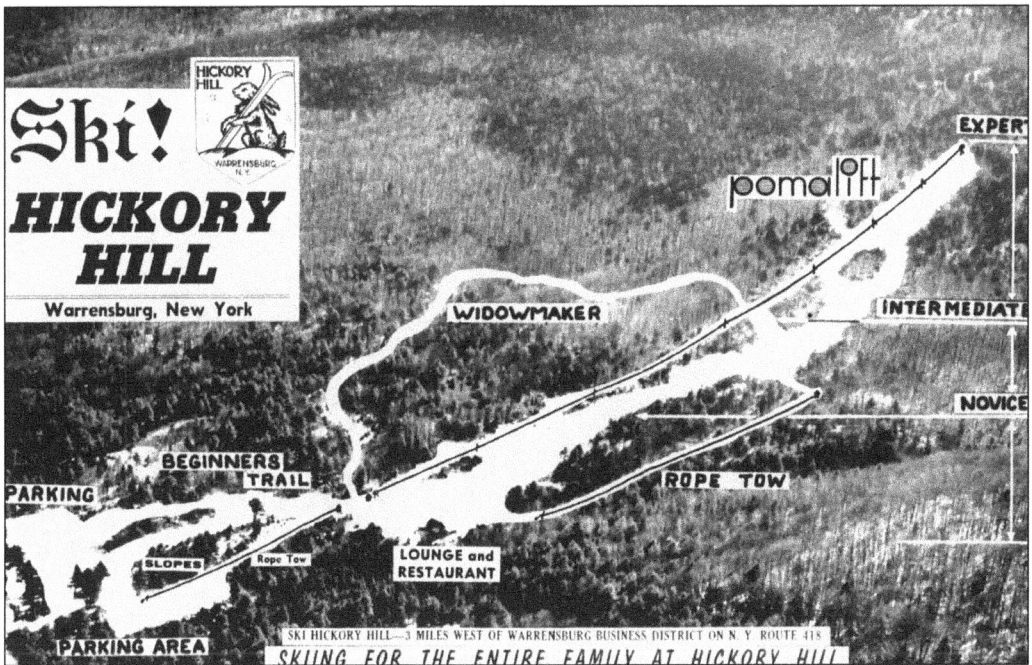

Hickory Hill ski area was first opened in 1946 by Fran and Hans Winbauer and Ken and Flo Bates. The slope is located on Pine Mountain, one of the Three Sisters Mountains. Skiing started with a rope tow, and all-day lift tickets cost $2. A second rope tow was installed after the second skiing season.

This view is of the Thurman Bridge and Sugarloaf Mountain. Stephen Griffin purchased 240 acres of land, which included Sugarloaf Mountain, from John Backus and moved from Dutchess County to this area in the spring of 1800. When he reached the "Bridge" (Warrensburg), he was unable to cross the Hudson River to his property due to unsafe ice and had to board at Jasper Duell's (location of Warren House). The first bridge was constructed here in 1836.

The railroad bridge was built in 1905 by the Delaware and Hudson Railroad Company, as part of the railroad extension from Thurman Station to Warrensburg. The extension was opened in early 1906. Sugarloaf Mountain is in the background. The section between Lewisville and the Thurman Bridge was often referred to as "Burnamsville."

Three

HUDSON STREET

Hudson Street veers off Main Street to the left, in front of the Woodward Block. Note the cast-iron water fountain in front, which was donated by Randolph McNutt and was present from the 1880s to the 1930s. (WMLH.)

Around 1839, Stephen Griffin purchased this property, which included a small house (currently the tavern and lounge). In the 1850s, Griffin added the Greek Revival front, and later (1920s) his granddaughter Grace Merrill relocated the back section from nearby (Griffin dining room). This is actually the oldest part of the house, dating back to 1812. For many years, the house was known as the Merrill Magee House but has recently reverted to the Griffin House, its original name.

The Woodward was owned by Charles and Edith Woodward and was in operation as a boardinghouse around 1940. Charles was a bank bookkeeper (most likely the Emerson National Bank). His father was Thomas Woodward, and his grandparents were John and Margaret Woodward (see page 78).

This house was built by John G. Smith around 1906. Smith constructed the first electric power plant in Warrensburg in 1894. The plant had a 140-horsepower generator with a capacity to power 1,000 lamps. In 1902, he contracted with the town to provide street lighting, which included 90–125 lights at $11 per light over a 10-year period. Power was on evenings and all day Tuesday for ironing.

Warren Co. Fair. Warrensburg, N.Y.

The fairgrounds were located in back of what is now Ashe's Hotel. The first annual Fair and Exhibition of the Warrensburgh Union Agriculture Society was held in September 1874 on the society's grounds. Horse racing, circuses, stock car races, and baseball were popular attractions, but other events, such as a rodeo and a marathon, were also held here. The grandstand burned on June 1, 1959.

This photograph was taken near the fairgrounds entrance in September 1914. Seen here are, from left to right, (first row) John Archer, Lillian McGann, Lottie Braley, Fred Hayes, Henry Griffin, Thomas J. Smith, Jean Kenyon, Emma Young, James McGann, and Harry Stockton; (second row) two unidentified, Lawrence Pratt, Orley Hazelton, Truman Brown, James Cunningham, Roscoe Stone, Edwin Robinson, and Thomas Woodward.

The Agricultural Hotel was purchased by Henry Ashe and his father, James Ashe, of Thurman in 1888. The property was purchased from Walter Baker, who owned and operated the Baker House next to the fairgrounds. Baker was a professional trainer of horses.

The Warren County Fair first started in Luzerne in 1857, moved to French Mountain settlement, and eventually Glens Falls. It was first held at the Warrensburg Fairgrounds in 1900 and ran until 1928. There was a track for horse racing and a grandstand that cost $25,000. The price for admission was $1 per family, which was good for the entire week of the fair.

ATTEND THE

WARREN COUNTY

FAIR

AT WARRENSBURGH, N. Y.

SEPT. 11-12-13-14

1906

EACH DAY INTERESTING. UP-TO-DATE EXHIBITS.
MANY NEW NOVELTIES. ALL DEPARTMENTS COMPLETE.

HENRY GRIFFINU, Pres. JAMES A. EMERSON, Vice-Pres. FRED J. HAYES, Secretary.
LOUIS E. REOUX, Treas. THOMAS J. SMITH, Rental Committee.

Echo Lake was originally named Bond's Pond after the first settler to the area, William Bond, who moved to lot No. 1 of Hyde Township around 1787. This has been a popular spot for swimming, fishing, and boating. Early inhabitants used the pond as a source of ice for summer refrigeration before electricity came to the village.

The Goody Shoppe,
Echo Lake Tavern,
Warrensburg, N.Y.

Echo Lake Tavern was situated on the north end of Echo Lake and incorporated in 1924. In its 1932 brochure, it advertised as an Adirondack Camp for adults. Cabins were rustic, with hot and cold showers and baths, electric lights, and private sanitary facilities. Activities included golf, swimming, canoeing, handball, baseball, basketball, volleyball, Ping-Pong, plays, musicals, and horseback riding. Rates were $25–$30 per week. Directors were Rebecca Nudell, Joseph Sarafite, and Louis Naftalison. In 1946, it was sold to Morey and Amy Stein, and it became part of Echo Lake Camp.

THE LODGE. ECHO LAKE TAVERN. WARRENSBURG N.Y.

Located on Echo Lake, Crooning Pines was a camp for adults established in 1926 that specialized in sports and recreation. The photograph above shows the office and library. Camps and cabins were located in a huge grove of white pines. It was owned by Eugene Lee and was in operation until the 1940s.

Indian Head Camp. Echo Lake. Warrensburgh. N. Y.

Indian Head Camp was located at Echo Lake and started in the 1930s by A. C. Emerson. The last owners were Bob and Lois Pasco, who ran it until around 1983. At this point, the Steins purchased the property, and it became part of Echo Lake Camp. There were 50 cabins.

Echo Lake Farm house was owned by Edward Noble and was located about one mile from the village, between the Hudson River and Echo Lake. A croquet grounds and tennis court were present. The parlor contained a fine piano and an Edison phonograph with 80 records. Rates were $6–$7 per week around 1912.

The Warrensburg Fish Hatchery was constructed by the New York State Conservation Commission around 1915. It was located on 50 acres of land on the Hudson River, which was originally the Lockwood Farm. The first superintendant was Sumner Cowden. Other superintendents were James Royce, Kenneth Nichols, Raymond Stone, and Irwin Annis. The hatchery is now owned by Warren County.

The New York State Department of Environmental Conservation Office (DEC) was built in 1963 and is located on Hudson Street Extension. It housed the divisions of lands and forest, fish and wildlife, operations, law enforcement, and environmental quality. The original log structure office is located in the village of Lake George on the corner of Route 9 and 9L and currently serves as a restaurant.

Cronin's Golf Course, originally Queen Village Golf Club and later Queen City Country Club, was established in 1930. Patrick J. Cronin, grandfather of the present owners, designed and operated the course in the early years with his partner Mark Cassidy. Later, in 1945, his son Bob Cronin took over the business. For the last 20 years, James and John Cronin have owned and operated this beautiful course along the banks of the Hudson River.

Four

EAST AND WEST
OF MAIN STREET

This is a view looking north along Elm Street, with the Union Free School on the right. Notice the road is still unpaved, and Library Avenue, which would be on the left side, has not been constructed yet.

An early location of the *Warrensburgh News* was just south of Pasco Park. It was established by John A. Morris, and the first issue was on January 17, 1878. Capt. M. N. Dickinson purchased the paper in 1881. John L. Tubbs and his wife are on the upper porch in this 1898 photograph. Standing on the bottom porch are, from left to right, Edward Beaupre, Myron Shaw, ? Martin, and John F. Ryan. (WMLH.)

A later home of the *Warrensburgh News* was located just west, across the street from the bandstand. This building was a two-story home built in 1899 by James Somerville, who was the owner and publisher of the newspaper beginning in 1890. The paper moved to this location in 1903. Tubbs, who was the newspaper editor from 1890 to 1932, lived with his family in the second-floor apartment. (RL.)

This residence was built in 1901 by Louis Weinman, who was a partner in the Empire Shirt Factory. The house became known for his son-in-law, Hart Joseph, who later owned it. About 1916, it became the home of Frank Smith, town supervisor, who died here when the house burned on June 22, 1931.

Richards Library was built in 1900 and financed by Clara Richards and Mary (Richards) Kellogg at a cost of $15,000. Plans were made by architect A. W. Fuller of Albany, and it was constructed of native limestone from the quarries of David Brown on County Mountain. It was gutted by fire in 1914 and rebuilt. The library has had only three librarians over its 109-year history: Mary Crandall, Jennie Cameron, and Sarah Farrar.

The original Warrensburgh Academy was built in 1854 with later additions (1875–1880) as shown in this photograph. The school was built by the stonemason Peter Buell. By 1859, it was completely paid for through the issuance of shares, which were valued at $12.50 each. The academy was torn down in 1898 to make room for the new Union Free School. (WMLH.)

The Warrensburg Union Free School was built in 1899 to replace the Warrensburgh Academy. The school was constructed of native stone by Jonah Hess of Johnstown. It was demolished in 1947 after construction of the school on James Street was completed.

The Presbyterian church was constructed in 1836 by Joseph Woodward in the Greek Revival style. It was extensively altered in 1887–1888 to a Queen Anne style, when the tower, a rear extension, and period decorative elements were added. The manse was built in 1899 by H. H. Hill. The original organ is a one-manual Jordine, installed in 1888.

This photograph is looking across the Osborne Bridge from the south side. In the background is Lavery's Store, which was built around 1880 by Halsey Herrick. Around 1899, it was sold to Charles Lavery. Other owners include Smith, Schloss, J. P. Reoner, and Bardwell. It was located on the lower end of Elm Street, across the road from what is now Riverside Gallery. (WCA.)

On June 21, 1921, the Warrensburg Fire Company was organized after the disastrous fire of the Warren House. With Fire Commissioner G. W. Dickinson presiding, 15 private citizens and the members of the town board constituted the first membership of the Warrensburg Fire Company. These original members were William Ticknor, Arthur Irish, Jay Griffin, Walter Pasco, William Varnum, William Hastings, Charles Brown, Milton Brown, George Hitchcock, M. J. Livingston, Earl Hitchcock, Joseph Hertz, M. L. Runner, William Condon, and John Ryan. These two photographs show the firehouse under construction in the summer of 1934. Note the original gatehouse to the Burhans estate in the background of the photograph above. (WMLH.)

The Warrensburg Central School was built in 1942 and opened the following year. The school district was formed in June 1938. It was necessary at that time to visit every house in the proposed district to get the petition signed. J. Russell White was the architect, and Mark Cassidy did the landscaping.

The Three Sisters Mountains from left to right are Pine, Bald, and the one on the far right, which is unnamed. The federal board of geographical names approved the change of Bald Mountain to Jimmie's Peak in honor of James Cameron, pioneer settler who came to the United States from Scotland in 1773. He is buried on the mountainside overlooking the scene of his labors. A marker was placed on the Warrensburg-Stony Creek Road in September 1940. (WMLH.)

The King's Addition was an early development east of Main Street. It was originally owned by Minerva King, but upon her death, it was subdivided into 159 lots by her sons Fred and H. Prior King in 1896. Although a few lots were on Main Street, most were between Hackensack Avenue and Grove Avenue (which is now Emerson Avenue).

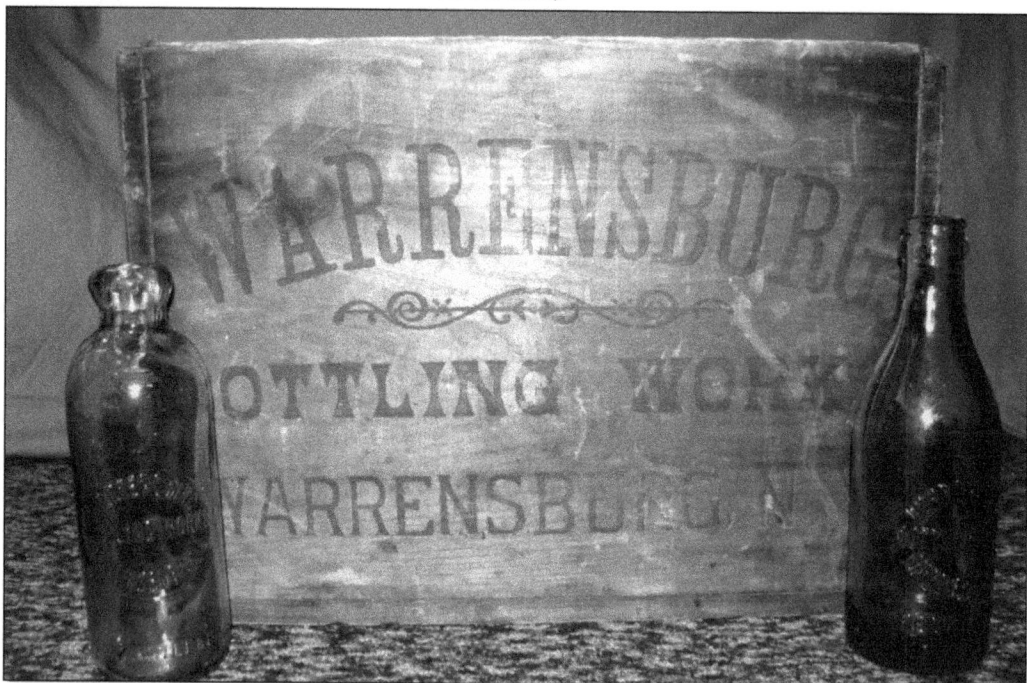

The Warrensburg Bottling Plant was located on Oak Street between Mountain and Adirondack Avenues. Fred M. Harrington purchased seven lots in the King's Addition in 1897. By 1898, the plant was in operation and continued until about 1922. A 1912 map shows two large buildings containing an office, two icehouses, a room for bottle storage, a sleeping room, and a wagon shed. There was a small pond nearby from which they obtained water.

This view is looking east on Mountain Avenue. The Fred King home is located in the left center of the photograph. Hackensack Mountain, which is 1,348 feet (410.87 meters) above sea level, is located in the background. Many of the aerial views of the town have been taken from the summit. In the 1960s, a forest fire destroyed much of the vegetation on the mountain.

The land for the almshouse, or poor house, was purchased in 1826, shortly after it became the county's responsibility to house the poor. The original structure was built around 1830. In 1865, the stone structure was constructed by Peter Buell, and in 1883, the old section was razed and a new wood addition added on. It would continue as the Warren County Home until 1979. It is located on Schroon River Road (formerly the Horicon Road). (WMLH.)

Schroon River Lodge, or Brown's farmhouse, was located on the Schroon River Road east of Warrensburg in the Vowers District. It was owned by Carlton Brown and his wife and was in operation from the mid-1920s to the early 1940s.

Camp Niaweh was a girls' camp established in 1931 and located about four miles outside Warrensburg on Schroon River Road. It bordered the Schroon River for over three miles. In a booklet dated 1948–1949, Barclay Bleecker and his wife were the directors, and the camp was open not only in the summer but also during the winter months. It was in operation until around 1958.

Five

WARRENSBURG TO CHESTERTOWN

The Toll Gate School House was located near the intersection of Routes 9 and 28, north of Warrensburg. This photograph dates from 1911. Seen here are, from left to right, (first row) Lawrence Raymond, Walter Wright, ? Merrithew, ? Morrison, ? Merrithew, and ? Morrison; (second row) ? Tripp, Ella Raymond, Cecelia Morrison, Gertrude Gehing, Jessie Merrithew, and Don Raymond; (third row) Dora Raymond, Nellie Raymond, Anna Morrison, Floyd Merrithew, Madoline Morrison, and ? Morrison.

Josiah Woodward and his family moved to Warrensburg from Connecticut and was the seventh family to settle in the Warrensburg area. His son Isaac Woodward established his home on what is now Pack Demonstration Forest around 1796. The building on the left is believed to be the original Woodward home. (WMLH.)

The early road from Warrensburg to Chestertown was filled with rocks and stumps and only passable by foot or horseback. Around 1850, the Warrensburgh-Chestertown Plank Road Company built a road of two-inch-thick hemlock timbers. Some of the timbers were sawn at the Woodward Mill near what is now Pack Demonstration Forest. This road allowed easier movement of logs and bark to area mills.

Pack Demonstration Forest was established in 1927 when Charles Lathrop Pack donated 2,500 acres of forestland to the College of Forestry at Syracuse. It would be used for forestry education, research, a summer camp, and as a demonstration area. Cliff Foster was the first manager and was followed later by Shelley Potter.

WARRENSBURG, N. Y.

The property that is now Pack Demonstration Forest was originally purchased around 1796 by the Josiah Woodward family, who were some of the earliest settlers to the area. Pictured are Margaret and John Woodward. John (1801–1883) was the grandson of Josiah Woodward. Margaret (1805–1894) was the daughter of Sam Somerville. Margaret and John are the source of the story of the Grandmother Tree, which is a large white pine located on the property. (Stewart Farrar collection.)

One version of the Grandmother Tree story goes as follows: John wanted to buy his wife Margaret a set of new dishes as an anniversary present but was short of cash. To pay for the dishes, he planned to cut down the old white pine to sell for lumber. When his wife found out about it, she told him she would rather go without the dishes than to allow him to cut the tree. Sarah Farrar notes that the family version of this story is that Margaret wanted a set of silver spoons but John would not cut the tree to buy the spoons. The story has passed down until the tree became known as the Grandmother Tree. Currently the tree is over 330 years old and 150 feet tall.

The Civilian Conservation Corps (CCC) camp was established when 90 men from Front Royal, Virginia, arrived at Pack Demonstration Forest on May 16, 1934, and established CCC Company No. 289. During the ensuing year, approximately 1,700 cords of wood were cut, 424 acres of forestland were improved, three miles of trail were built, 200 acres were cleared of blister rust, and four bridges were built. The photograph shows a fireplace from one of the original structures.

Tripp Lake House was built in the early 1900s by R. C. Fox. It was located on the west side of the lake and touted free boats for fishing on a privately owned lake, which was controlled by the owner. Rates were $5–$6 per week. It was known to be in operation from 1910 through 1915.

Green Mansions was in operation before 1929. It is located on Tripp Lake, off Route 9 between Warrensburg and Chestertown. Early owners were Lena Barish and Sam Garlen. The nine-hole golf course was opened in 1930. Rates at this time were $32 to $37.50 per week. Green Mansions is still in operation.

GREEN MANSIONS

TRIPP LAKE LODGE, CHESTERTOWN, N.Y. 13A.

Tripp Lake Lodge was located off Route 9 between Warrensburg and Chestertown and opened around 1926 with R. C. Fox and Son as proprietors. It was noted for fishing and boating on Tripp Lake, which was well stocked with fish. It "catered to the better class of tourist." Music and dancing were also a highlight.

INTERIOR OF DININGROOM, TRIPP LAKE LODGE, CHESTERTOWN N.Y. 5C.

Six

LOCAL CAMPS AND RESORTS

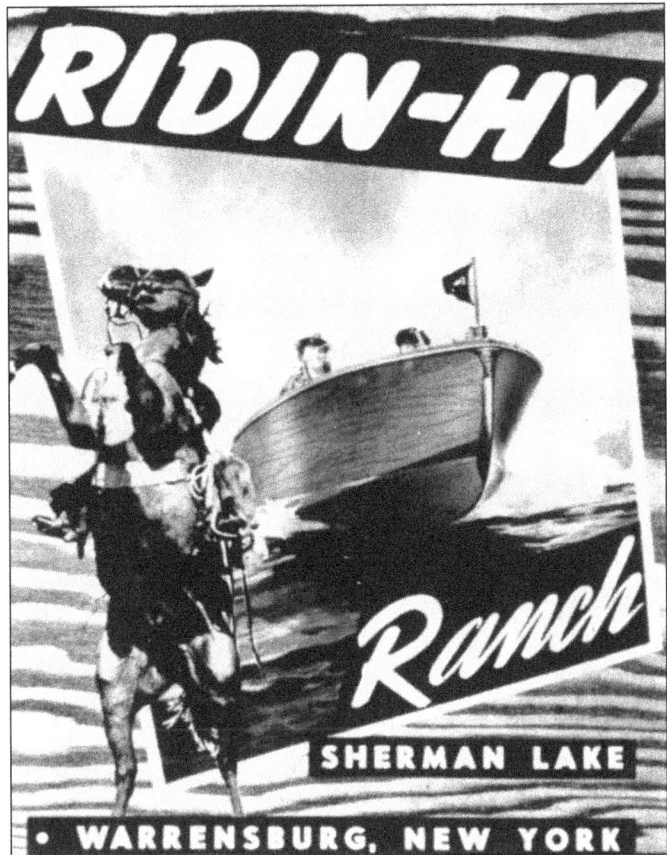

Ridin-Hy was established in 1943 by Edward Carstens. The site was originally a girls' summer camp, Camp Arcady in the Pines. A 1951 brochure notes the magnificent Paradise Lodge, which was built in 1948 and constructed of native pine logs. Many activities are noted, including aquaplaning and speedboating. In 1976, a rodeo was begun, and in 1977, a ski slope and winter activities were added. Current owners are Sue (Carstens) and Andy Beadnell, who have been operating it since 1970.

Hi:...

We're Esther and Jack Arehart!

We welcome you and join you in the fun at our . . .

THOUSAND ACRES RANCH RESORT

You Arrive!

The special charm of

1000 Acres

warm friendliness
makes you feel at
home.
YOU'RE IN!

Member
New York State Hotel Association
American Hotel Association

AAA

Thousand Acres was located on the Hudson River off Route 418, southwest of Warrensburg. It was first established in 1919 and catered to men and women seeking escape, relaxation, and outdoor activity. The 1,000 Acres Ranch Resort was started by Esther and John E. (Jack) Arehart in 1942. The first rodeo was held in 1949. It was often called the "Cadillac of Ranching." In 1968, the ranch was left to John's son Jack, and the ranch remains in the ownership of the Arehart family. Some of the early activities were swimming, horseback riding, corral games, horseshoe pitching, archery, rifle range, billiards, shuffleboard, boating, fishing, tennis, and hiking. The view below shows an early view of the main gate to the ranch.

MAIN GATE AT THOUSAND ACRES RANCH, STONY CREEK, N.Y.

Boulder Greens Dude Ranch was located on Emerald Lake northwest of Warrensburg. Alan and Myrtle Mitcheltree opened the ranch in 1938 and operated it through 1943. Rates in 1942 were $29 to $35 per week, and the ranch boasted 1,000 acres, 25 horses, 40 bedrooms, 12 separate cabins, a new Bell telephone, and accommodations for 80 people.

Around 1944, Boulder Greens Dude Ranch became Sun Canyon Dude Ranch. The owners were Myrtle Mitcheltree and Robert Venton. Robert Venton had a 25 percent interest in Hidden Valley, which he traded to Mitcheltree to become sole owner of Sun Canyon. In 1962, he sold it to country music singer Cathy Carr and Ron Cash. Accommodations were possible for 150 guests, and 65 horses were available for riding. The ranch burned in 1965.

Hidden high up in the Adirondacks on top of French Hill, (altitude 2000 feet), and guarded safely by old Crane Mountain, nestles SKI-HI RANCH.

"SKI-HI" is completely surrounded by the 3,000,000 acre State Park which affords miles of mountain trails for horseback riding and unlimited opportunities for the hiker. For the fisherman are secluded mountain streams and many hidden, sparkling lakes. All other out o' door sports and games are provided --- one will not lack for wholesome activity.

In 1931, Vern and Lulu Walter bought property from Thomas Nichols and started what may have been the first dude ranch in the eastern United States. Ski-Hi Ranch opened the following year and was located near Crane Mountain at an elevation of 2,000 feet. In 1947, the ranch was sold to Harry and Mozelle Richter, who ran it until 1964. Activities included swimming, mountain climbing, archery, rifle practice, fishing, horseback riding, rodeos, and square dancing.

Circle B Ranch is located on Friends Lake Road and was originally the Fred Carpenter farm. The ranch was started by Spencer LaFlure in 1953 as the Circle R. In 1960, Mae and Joe Boggia bought the ranch and renamed it the Circle B. The ranch includes six cottages and is currently being run by the Boggia family.

BREEZY KNOLL
Warrensburg N Y
Private Lake · Cabins
6 miles north of Lake George

Breezy Knoll was a 12-room cottage with five rustic one-room bungalows located near Warrensburg. There were numerous trails for hiking, as well as space for tennis and croquet. Breezy Knoll was in operation in the 1930s and into the 1950s and was "an ideal spot for those who seek quiet and rest." It was first operated by Jennie Bennett as a boardinghouse and then later by J. Hatheway and Bill and Gladys Reimers.

MOOSE MOUNTAIN LODGE

Moose Mountain Lodge is known to have been in operation from 1932 through 1955, with George and Margaret Drexel as owners. Outdoor activities included swimming, tennis, croquet, horseshoes, and boating. For indoor recreation, one could try shuffleboard, Ping-Pong, and square dancing. Horses could be rented nearby for horseback riding. This was a favorite haven for German guests.

Skye Farm Camps is located on Sherman Lake. It was begun as a summer youth camp in the 1940s to serve the United Methodist Churches of the Troy Annual Conference. It runs a horse-training camp in conjunction with Circle B Ranch in Chestertown.

Forest Lake Camp was established in 1923 by Harold Confer. By 1954, Phillip Confer and his wife were directors. It was originally an Adirondack Camp for boys 6–16, with three program levels, junior, intermediate, and senior, and an eight-week session starting in early July. The camp was located five miles north of Warrensburg on the east side of Route 9.

Seven

PEOPLE

One of the most noted sons of Warrensburg was Floyd Bennett. In 1917, he enlisted in the United States Navy, served as an aviation mechanic, and in 1925, was assigned to Lt. Comdr. Richard E. Byrd's naval aviation group. He soon became Byrd's close friend and personal pilot. Together they planned and carried out a flight over the North Pole for which both men were awarded the Medal of Honor. Bennett died in 1928.

Early in his career, B. P. Burhans was employed by Palen and Company in Greene County and eventually became a partner (1831). In 1836, he moved to Warrensburg and purchased the interest of Mr. Quackenbush in the leather manufacturing business. By 1860 (with son Frederick), the business became known as B. P. Burhans and Son. He was colonel of the 3rd Regiment of the New York State Militia and elected as member of the assembly (1842).

Stephen Griffing was the owner of the Adirondack House from 1838 to 1847. He served as town supervisor in 1857–1858 and in 1869. In 1874, he was elected assemblyman, and from 1834 to 1866, he was part owner in the Emerson sawmill. He began lumbering around 1866 and eventually built the Oregon and Griffin tanneries. In 1882, he sold these interests to the Morgan Lumber Company, which eventually became part of International Paper Company.

Peletiah Richards (1786–1870), an early settler to Warrensburg (1802), owned a distillery south of the village. He served as sheriff of Warren County (1820), Warrensburg's supervisor (1830 and 1838), New York State assemblyman (1842), and charter member of the Warrensburg IOOF Lodge (1857). In addition, he was instrumental in the construction of the plank road from Glens Falls to Chestertown. He also was an early director of the Glens Falls Insurance Company and the Glens Falls National Bank. (RL.)

Joseph Russell (1800–1875) was active in business and politics. He was part owner of the Warren House (1860s) and Emerson Sawmill (1840s). In 1829, 1831–1834, and 1839 he served as town supervisor and was Warren County sheriff in 1834. He served as representative to Congress in 1845–1847 and was a charter member of Warrensburg Lodge No. 425. He was also on the original board of directors for the First National Bank of Glens Falls. (RL.)

James A. Emerson was educated in the Warrensburgh Academy. He owned the Leland House and became president or vice president of the Emerson Bank, Empire Shirt Company, Warrensburgh Woolen Mill, and Schroon River Pulp and Paper Company. He served as member of the New York State Senate, 1907–1918, and was an opponent of prohibition in 1918. He was called "wringing wet" (in contrast to prohibition advocates, who were "desert dry"). His son Albert L. is on his lap. (WMLH.)

Louis W. Emerson graduated from the Warrensburgh Academy. Like his brother James, he was engaged in the lumber, banking, and manufacturing business and was a delegate to the Republican National Conventions in 1888, 1892, and 1896. He served as a member of the New York State Senate from 1890 to 1893 and was elected as a Republican to the 56th and 57th Congress (1899–1903). (WMLH.)

Albert L. Emerson was the son of James W. Emerson. His early education was in the public schools of Warrensburg, and he later matriculated at Dartmouth College. Albert was proprietor of the Leland House, cashier of the Emerson Bank, president of the Warrensburgh Woolen Company, vice president of the A. C. Emerson Company, vice president of the Schroon River Paper and Pulp Company, and director of the Tait Paper and Color Industry. (WMLH.)

The Bear-Waller Hunting Club was formed in 1909. Members had to be 21 years old and a resident of Warrensburg. Dues were $12 per year, and membership was limited to a maximum of 12. The camp was located at Sawyer's Clearing on the Sacandaga River near Oregon. Charter members were L. E. Crandall, J. P. Gabel, Dr. J. E. Goodman, Charles Green, James Guyette, Thurston Kenyon, Orlin Magee, E. C. Manzer, Louis Manzer, H. C. Smith, Lee Stockton, and Dr. W. F. Wilkinson.

This photograph of the Warrensburg Fire Company officers was taken around 1940. Seen here are, from left to right, (first row) William Ticknor, Herrick Osborne, Howard Hull, and Louis Crandall; (second row) Loran Hoffman, Arthur Fish, Joseph Anselmo, William Hastings, Edward Frye, Sig Wachter, and Frank Bisbe. Note that the current (when the photograph was taken) officers are in uniform.

The first Warrensburg High School football team was organized in 1905 with Ralph Smith as captain and Arthur Adams as manager. The name chosen was the Athletics. The first game was played at the fairgrounds where Warrensburg defeated Fort Edward 7-0. They are, from left to right, (first row) Mead, T. Hurley, Heinerman, Carrie the mascot, and Adams; (second row) Somerville, Stockton, Heath, Smith, and Ryan; (third row) Kenyon (assistant coach), Prosser, Patterson, O'Neil, and Dr. D. H. Hurley (coach).

The Maplewoods baseball team photograph was taken around 1912. Seen here are, from left to right, (first row) Cassius Logan, Albert Bennett, Maurice O'Connor, Lawrence Woodward, and Albert Emerson (mascot); (second row) Marshall Burt, John O'Connor, Stewart Farrar, Lee Orton, Earl Herrick, and Clarence Potter.

Members of the Green Rangers Rifle Team are shown in this photograph taken around 1955. They are, from left to right, (first row) Roscoe Hastings, Mary Carpenter, Sue Alger, Jennie Hastings, and Dick Kline; (second row) Judd Smith, Milo "Harry" Alger, Grant Smith, Chuck Wheeler, Judd Smith Jr., and Mark Webster. (Charles Wheeler.)

In February 1983, coach George Khoury broke the New York State record for career coaching victories (515) in a basketball game versus Luzerne. He spent his entire career, which started in 1947, coaching at Warrensburg. He was a graduate of Ithaca College. Above are Dan Sheehan, coach, and Don Hastings with the 1961 Adirondack League Football Trophy. The photograph is from the 1962 Hackensack, Warrensburg Central School yearbook.

Warrensburg schoolteachers are shown in this photograph taken in 1935. Seen here are, from left to right, (first row) Louise Tubbs, Ruby Squires, Kathleen Baker, Evelyn Brown, Ruth McCrae, and Armine Gurney; (second row) Elizabeth Hurley, Anna Frost, Imogene Thayer, Faustine Bennett, Ada Guiles, Minnie (Mary) Crandall, Hannah Bilodeau, Grace Hastings, Lucy Kendrew, and Regina Orton; (third row) Henry Cameron (custodian), Frank Cameron, Jenniemay Monroe, J. Harold Ripton (principal), Robert Swan, and Arthur Schrader (custodian). (WMLH.)

John Tubbs was born in Oneida Lake in 1861. When he was two, his family moved to Glens Falls and then Lake George. At age 19, he owned a bowling alley that he traded for half interest as editor of the *Lake George Mirror*. Later he became editor of the *Warrensburgh News*, a position that he held for 40 years. He was also an accomplished musician with the violin, piano, organ, bass fiddle, and tuba.

This photograph of shirt factory workers was taken around 1900. The numbered men are as follows: Burt Fuller (1), Percy Hall (2), Charlie Green (3), Charlie Fuller (4), George ? (5), Frank Trip (6), Louis Putnam (7), Arthur Hayes (8), Frank Boprey (9), Miles Towns (10), Forest Moore (11), Add Haight (12), ? Beswick (13), Jim Somerville (14), Harry Saunders (15), Hugh Owens (16), Stuart Haight (17), Morg Lavall (18), Godfrey Hewit (19), Forest Smith (20), unidentified (21), Dennis Church (22), unidentified (23), unidentified (24), and Bob Davis (25).

The Warrensburg Band members pose for a photograph in 1931. Seen here are, from left to right, (first row) Fred King, Harry Young, Gilbert Weaver, Walt Weaver, Wilson Montena, and Prof. R. Price; (second row) Ellwood Vickery, Lew Crandall, Jack Lynn, Heyward Street, Charles Briggs, Loren Davis, and Charles Wade; (third row) A. J. Woodward, Wallace Austin, and Ray Pasco; (fourth row) Dr. Wilkenson, Marshall Burt, and James Keays Jr.; (fifth row) John Tubbs, Ernest Rist, and Larry Wallace. (WMLH.)

The board of education of the Warrensburg Central School in 1942 consisted of the individuals seen here. They are, from left to right, (first row) Albert L. Emerson, Walter H. Pasco, and Don H. Cameron; (second row) Howard E. Hull (president), Ralph M. Brown, Nathan Gifford (superintendant principal), and Charles H. Brown (clerk).

Eight

THE GLEN AND
FRIENDS LAKE

MAIN STREET, THE GLEN, N.Y. NO. 3.

Located just west of the Glen Bridge on the Hudson River, the Glen forms the corner of three townships, Warrensburg, Johnsburg, and Thurman. The Delaware and Hudson Railroad train station was located here from 1870 to 1939 and was where most people disembarked for Friends Lake, Chestertown, and points east.

The Grove Hotel was located near the railroad station. In the 1920s, it was owned by James McPhillips, and a 1920s brochure noted that a stringed orchestra entertained the guests with concert music during the dinner hour. It was originally the home of Robert Gilchrest, who engineered the construction of the bridge at Washburn Eddy.

GLEN GARTH, THE GLEN, N.Y. 27.

Glen Garth is located at the top of the hill in back of where the train depot used to be. A stairway led from the train station to the boardinghouse. Walkways on the grounds were packed dirt and were swept daily to keep seeds and such from germinating and growing. It is now the private residence of John and Jenny Taylor.

APPROACH TO GLENGARTH, THE GLEN, N.Y. No. 5.

The Glen Bridge was the boundary line for the towns of Warrensburg, Johnsburg, Chester, and Thurman when it was first built in 1816. As a result of melting ice and snow, the bridge was swept away in 1843 and again in January 1903. Chester took over Warrensburg's share of the bridge when the boundary lines were changed in 1860. The replacement in 1903 was the iron bridge in the photograph below. (RL.)

These two views are looking north (above) and south (below) along the Hudson River from the Glen. Note the train tracks in the north photograph. The Glen Station was a popular "stepping off" place for tourists going to Friends Lake and Chestertown.

This is a view looking south from the porch of the Goodman Hotel and shows the pulp and paper mill started by a stock company, which included Amasa Howland, Fred D. Howland, and John J. Cunningham and was eventually run by the McPhillips Brothers from 1913 to 1916. It was located adjacent to the railroad tracks, on the east side. The mill capacity was to be 25 tons per day. Dams were part of the original proposal but never constructed.

Friends Lake is three miles long and about a half mile wide. It is located north of Warrensburg and about two miles from the Glen. Originally it was called Atateka Lake, which means "friendly waters." It is truly a "Gem of the Adirondacks."

The McPhillips Hotel was located on a bluff on the southwest end of Friends Lake and began operation about 1888. Early on it was known as the Troy House. A 1930s brochure details the presence of a ball field, tennis court, and croquet grounds. The house and cottages were lit with electricity and came with telephone and telegraph connections with all points. It operated as a resort well into the 1960s.

The Atateka Club began operation around 1918 and continued into the mid-1930s. It was run by the Mahoney brothers and could accommodate 100 guests. The Marion House, which was started around 1904, served as an annex to the club. Dancing, boating, bathing, fishing, hunting, tennis, and baseball were listed activities. Saddle horses, automobile rental, and a telephone were also available.

The Baldwin House was open from the 1890s until around 1917. It was built by William Baldwin, with his son, Harry, serving as manager. It catered to sportsmen and "lovers of nature." A 1901 advertisement noted that it was two and a half miles from the (railroad) station, could accommodate 30 guests, and had a livery. Rates were $7 per week.

The Pines was in operation during the early to mid-1900s. It was owned by E. E. Carpenter. An early brochure noted "Sanitary arrangements are all that can be desired. The natural drainage of the hills and slopes is so complete, that malaria influences from any cause cannot exist. There are no unwholesome or unsavory odors from any source."

106

Valentine's on Atateka Lake, Adirondack Mountains.

Valentines was originally owned by E. E. Valentine, with R. E. Valentine as manager. It was located on the east side of Friends Lake and began operation around 1891. Around 1908, it was rebuilt to include a new water system with toilets and baths. It could accommodate 100 guests. In 1946, it was being run by Neil and Ann Sullivan. Weekly rates were $39 to $40. Entertainment included tennis, croquet, Ping-Pong, archery, dancing, and fishing.

The Balsam House, which was originally Valentines, was in business in the late 1940s and 1950s. At this time, it was owned by Herman and Suzanne Lutz. In 1982, actress Mary Frann stayed here to get ideas for *Newhart*. An explosion in 1994 did extensive damage to the building.

The Friends Lake House was in business by 1896 and owned by Daniel Murphy. In 1898, a first-class baseball field was a special attraction of this house and was the scene of many spirited baseball games between this and the neighboring hotels. In September 1912, the hotel was destroyed by fire. It was rebuilt, and the name was changed to the Atateka Hotel, which continued operation into the 1950s.

HOTEL ATATEKA AND COTTAGES ON FRIENDS LAKE – CHESTERTOWN, N. Y.
8355

The Friends Lake Inn began operation around 1901. It was owned by William Murphy. A 1920s brochure notes modern conveniences of acetylene gas, bathroom, toilets and sanitary plumbing, and long-distance telephone. Guides were available for rowing or fishing. Rates were $15 per week or $4 per day. It is still in business and located near the north end of the lake.

The Lake View House began operation before 1896. It was originally owned by Thomas Murphy. In 1904, Ella Murphy took over the operation and ran the business until the late 1930s. An early brochure indicates accommodations for 75 guests, electric lights, modern bath, spring beds, and a large parlor for dancing. The house was located on the western shore of the lake.

Fine, Fine, Weather good, Joe. track fast io bets.

Lake View Lodge r Cottage, Friends Lake, The Glen NY.

Lake View Lodge was in operation before World War II (1939 and later). It was located on the west side of Friends Lake and run by Mrs. Thomas McPhillips. An early brochure notes that the lodge and cottage have daily mail, telephone, and wire services. Also they had been entirely renovated and electrified throughout.

Originally this area was a summer camp owned by G. A. Rogers. The hotel was located on a knoll, which commanded an entire view of the lake. Facilities included a private beach and boats. Hunting and fishing parties were welcome. Hotel Rogers was known to be in operation from 1948 to 1958. In 1959, William Carlozzi started the Roger's Housekeeping Cottages.

Nine

CHESTERTOWN

Bird's Eye View of Chestertown,
Adirondack Mountains, N. Y.

The town of Chester was established in 1799 and set off from the town of Thurman, which was then a part of Washington County. Originally it was named Wabir and was later called Chester Four Corners. It is not clear where the name Chester originates from. The town's west border is the Hudson River, and the Schroon River forms the border on the east.

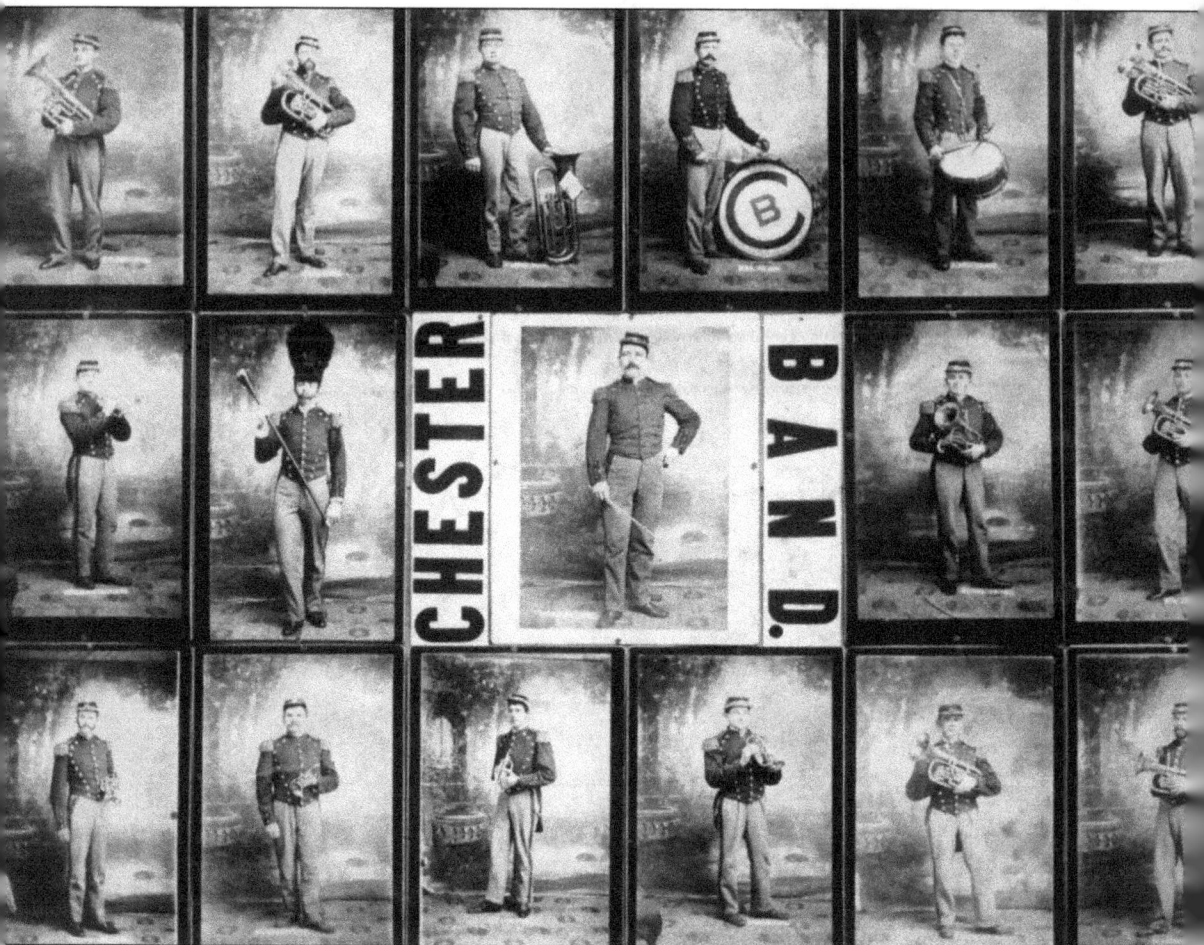

The Chester Band was famous around Warren County during the early part of the 20th century. Members dressed in blue uniforms. The band held concerts every Sunday night and gave concerts in the park on weekends during the summer. The photograph is by J. F. Holley and courtesy of Mark Walp of Friends Lake Books.

Shadrack Mead was the first proprietor of the Rising House, which was built in 1835. In 1896, it was being run by Mrs. H. Rising. Rates were $10 per week, and accommodations were for 75 guests. Advertisements mention good fishing and hunting, with guides available. In 1898, it was being heated by steam throughout. In the early 1920s, J. O'Connell became proprietor and ran the hotel into the 1950s.

The Chester House was built in the mid-1800s and had a capacity of 150 guests. In 1869, it was purchased by M. H. Downs, whose family ran it until the 1940s. A golf course was present around 1900, and guides were furnished for guests. Springwater came from the top of Panther Mountain. In the 1930s, guests included Norman Rockwell, John Sanford, George Eastman, and J. S. Wooley. The hotel was torn down in 1955.

The White House was built in 1865 by Charles Faxon as a homestead and later became the Panther Mountain House. Faxon was the owner/operator of the local tannery from 1856 through 1893. He was regarded as one of the kings of the logging industry and a leading industrialist. He also owned the local gristmill and improved the Chester Water Works, as well as being one of the original incorporators of the United States Leather Company. (TCHO.)

The high school was built on Main Street in 1913. It contained four classrooms and taught a variety of subjects to grades 7 through 12. In 1935, the school activities were moved to the newly built Chestertown Central School, and it became a glove assembly factory, then later an antique showroom and finally offices for the town of Chester from 1960 to 2001. Currently it is the Main Street Ice Cream Parlor and Restaurant, owned by Bruce and Helena Robbins.

The Panther Mountain House was built around 1865 by Charles Faxon as a homestead. In 1925, it was purchased by Walter Wertime and turned into a hotel. It had modern appliances and steam heat and could accommodate 50 guests for $25 per week. In March 1941, it was destroyed by fire. The current Panther Mountain House was rebuilt shortly after this. The photograph at the right is by photographer Itsuzo Sumy.

Vetter's Hardware store was first started in 1830 by Ezra Smith. It went through various ownerships until 1881 when Fred Vetter purchased the store. The retail hardware store also sold plumbing and heating supplies, as well as sporting goods. A tinsmith's shop was located on the second floor. In 1910, his sons Earl and Ralph joined him in the business. Later Ralph's son Frederick succeeded him and ran the store until 1969. (TCHO.)

Early owners of Janser's Drug Store were Sanford, Dolan, and Dessert. The store was built before 1900. Walter Janser bought the business in 1906, and Roy Boles began working here in 1915. A new soda fountain was purchased in 1916. (TCHO.)

The Kettenbach brothers, William and Cyrus, ran a general store in this building from 1888 until the 1940s. At one time, the IOOF Lodge met on the second floor. After the Kettenbach store closed, the A&P Tea Company occupied the store until 1958. At this point the U.S. Postal Service took occupancy until 1986. (TCHO.)

Riverside Drive extends westerly from Main Street and passes the industrial development that would occur near Chestertown, including the gristmill and tannery. This photograph shows Riverside Drive at the west end near the intersection with Knapp Hill Road. The building in the photograph was at one time Perry's boardinghouse and is still present. This view is looking east toward the village.

The gristmill was located west of the village near the millpond. It was originally built around 1800 by Jehiel Fox. After the mill burned in 1841 under the management of Alonzo Towsley, it was rebuilt by John Ranson, who later sold it to Charles H. Faxon in 1849. The mill was capable of grinding 30,000 bushels of wheat per year. Later it was owned by Dr. Howard Swan. (TCHO.)

The tannery was constructed in 1849 and was originally Robertson, Faxon and Company. By 1865, Faxon had bought out the other interests and became sole owner. In 1869, the tannery burned but was promptly rebuilt. In 1882, Charles' son, William, became a partner. It would close in 1898 after five years as the United States Leather Company. Up to 50 people were employed, tanning 24,000 to 30,000 hides to produce 300,000 pounds of sole leather.

Chestertown, N.Y.   Cowan Photo.

The Catholic church was purchased from the Methodists in 1867 and remodeled for $1,000. In 1885, there were 30 families in the church. Patrick McAveigh, John McPhillips, and Timothy Murphy were the first trustees. The structure shown was torn down in 1934 and replaced with the current stone church.

The Methodists began meeting in Chestertown in 1830. The first church was located at the corner of Knapp Hill and the Friends Lake Road. In 1835, a new church was built, which was sold and in 1867 became the Catholic church. The building at right was constructed in 1867 at a cost of $6,000. The spire in this photograph was removed in the early 1900s because it was considered dangerous but was then replaced in 1965 and again in 2007.

Community Church Chestertown, N.Y. A259

119

The Episcopal church was built in 1884 at a cost of $2,500. Rev. Clement Whipple had taken charge the previous year. In 1887, he was followed by Rev. Joseph Zorn and later Rev. Alfred Taylor. The year 1891 noted 58 communicants at the Chestertown church.

Swan's Pond, now Cunningham Pond, is located south of the village behind the Chester Rural Cemetery on Cunningham Loop. The Swan brothers, Frank and Richard, owned a sawmill and ran a lumber business for 42 years in this location. In the late 1920s, Richard became the sole owner of the business.

120

The 1964 national Christmas tree came from Landon Hill, three miles north of the village. The tree was planted by George Robinson and his son Beul, who had moved to the Landon Road area in the 1880s. The tree was a white spruce and was the first national Christmas tree to come from New York State.

The Green Lantern Inn is the house immediately south of the current town hall in Chestertown. In the late 1940s, it was owned by John and Martha Gibbs, who gave it the name of Green Lantern Inn. Green Mansions apparently raised some concern about the name being close to theirs, and the Gibbs changed the name to 7 Elms.

The Grand View Inn was located just south of the village, on the west side of Route 9. In the 1920s, it was operated by Daniel Shugrue. It was a modern structure with all improvements. Accommodations were for 100 people with boating, bathing, and fishing activities. Around 1928, it was being run by Jack Mullarkey and had a practice golf course, tennis court, and dance hall.

Maple Grove Farm began operation around 1910 with Mrs. Henry Tabor as the proprietor. The farm was located on White Lake and touted good roads for bicycling and automobiling. Good fishing, hunting, boating, and bathing were available. Accommodations were for 25 guests with rates of $7–$8 per week. Prior to this, the farm was known as the Balm Gilead Cottage.

The McAveigh House was operated by James McAveigh and began operation around 1912. Accommodations were limited, and rates were $8–$12 per week. Noted were the excellent hunting, driving, boating, bathing, fishing, tennis courts, and "gratuitous instruction in dancing." Around 1939, Hixson Wilson became owner.

Mills Adirondack Camp was started in 1922 by Dr. W. Hough Mills and his wife (of Syracuse) and was in operation until around 1940. It could accommodate up to 50 pupils and accepted girls 5–20 years of age and boys 5–12 years old. Dancing, swimming, canoeing, tennis, baseball, croquet, and hiking were summer activities. The cost was $275 per session.

123

Mountain Spring Camp, Chestertown, N.Y. 10C.

The "N" at Mountain Spring Camp was a large "N" on the side of the hill of the camp. The camp was started around 1932 by Edith Nichols. It was located on a large private estate on Route 9 and contained marked trails for climbing and hiking, as well as other activities of hunting, tennis, and fishing. It had furnished bungalows for rent. Also noted was a short drive to four golf courses.

Glen Rose Inn, miles south of Chestertown, N.Y. 442

The Glen Rose Inn was located on Route 9 just south of the current NAPA store. It was a bar and grill that featured dancing and was in operation from around 1945 into the 1950s. Currently it is used for apartments.

Camp White Owl was located on the Darrowsville Road, which is off Route 9 south of Chestertown. It was also known as Jen's Den and George's Hideaway and was a bar, which served light meals. Currently it is a private residence near the Red Truck Clay Works.

Stewarts Mountain View House was a family resort located off White Schoolhouse Road, three miles from Chestertown. An early brochure lists activities of swimming, boating, horseshoes, badminton, mountain climbing, and horseback riding at a neighboring dude ranch. It could accommodate up to 60 guests in either the two-story main house or the nearby cottages.

BIBLIOGRAPHY

Beers Atlas of Warren County, New York. New York: Charles Hart, 1876.

DeGarmo, Todd, et al. *Amusements, Summer Camps and Dude Ranches*. New York: Crandall Public Library, 1997.

DeMille, George E. *Adirondack Missions*. New York: self-published, c. 1974.

Fish, Caroline. *History of the Town of Chester*. Chestertown, New York: Civic Directory of Chester, Historical Society of the Town of Chester, 1969.

Fisher, Marie H. *North from the Plank Road Bridge, A Sketch Book of Warrensburgh*. New York: self-published, 1974.

Glimpses of the Past. Historical Society of the Town of Chester, 1987.

Greenwood, Bea. *Reflections and Recollections of the Town With a Past*. New York: Greenwood Publishing Company, 2002.

Kudish, Michael. *Where Did the Tracks Go in the Eastern Adirondacks?* New York: Purple Mountain Press, 2009.

Smith, H. P. *History of Warren County*. New York: D. Mason and Company, 1885.

Souvenir Edition of the Warrensburgh News. New York: 1898.

Tubbs, Margaret Louise. *Legacy to Warrensburg*. New York: self-published, 1978.

Vogal, Pam. *Our Waters Potable and Notable, Warren County, New York*. New York, self-published, 1977.

WARRENSBURGH HISTORICAL SOCIETY

The Warrensburgh Historical Society (WHS) was founded in 1973 and obtained its charter from the New York State education department the following year. Around 1983, the society became inactive.

In April 1996, a group of Warrensburg citizens met with past officers of the WHS with the objective to revitalize the society by establishing a board of directors, electing officers, and applying to have the WHS charter renewed. Bylaws and a system for accepting general membership were then established.

The goals of the WHS are to help preserve the community history through historically oriented social activities; support existing programs and organizations consistent with the society's goals; compose and publish material of general historic interest; and finally to collect, preserve, and display artifacts of historical interest.

In November 1996, the first quarterly newsletter was published. This publication has been provided to society members and village citizens for the last 13 years. In the summer of 1997, the WHS initiated its first fund-raiser, the Sticky Wicket. This fund-raiser is an afternoon picnic with competitive croquet matches held at the Warren County Fish Hatchery. The event has continued every summer since the inaugural event. The society continues to promote the local history through guest speakers, artifact show and tell, and fall graveyard walks. Recent major activities include fund-raising and restoration of the bicentennial mural, painted by Eva Cockcroft in 1976. Also the summer of 2009 saw the reopening of the Warrensburgh Museum of Local History. The museum was founded in 1975, and the WHS, with the support of the town government, has spent the last five years renovating, reorganizing, and recataloging a collection of more than 5,000 artifacts.

For more information go to the WHS Web site, whs12885.org.

Visit us at
arcadiapublishing.com

www.ingramcontent.com/pod-product-compliance
Lightning Source LLC
Chambersburg PA
CBHW080553110426
42813CB00006B/1296